UPDATED EDITION

Five Nights at Freddy's

OFFICIAL GUIDE

T0021961

SECURITY

BREACH

FILES

EVERYTHING YOU NEED TO KNOW ABOUT
THE LATEST FIVE NIGHTS AT FREDDY'S
GAME SECURITY BREACH, NOW WITH
"RUIN" DLC CONTENT!

Five Nights at Freddy's™

SECURITY BREACH FILES

SCHOLASTIC INC.

CONTENTS

3:00 a.m.

4:00 a.m.

5:00 a.m.

6:00 a.m.

RUIN

FREDDY FAZBEAR

ARE YOU READY?

Woo-aah! A whole afternoon at Freddy Fazbear's Mega Pizzaplex! Awesome stage shows, wicked rides, arcade games, popcorn, and pizza. Yummy! What starts as a day to remember for one wide-eyed schoolkid, Gregory, turns into a freakish nightmare he'll want to forget.

Locked inside the Pizzaplex after hours, Gregory must stay safe until morning, avoiding the attention of security guard Vanessa who knows he's sneaking around somewhere. Vanessa is not the only presence Gregory has to worry about, however. Malfunctioning animatronic attractions have joined the hunt. If they catch up with Gregory it's . . . well, it's GAME OVER!

With the whole place otherwise empty, Gregory pads silently around the Pizzaplex, where you can almost smell the soda-soaked carpets and popcorn—meets—hot dog funk. This is no place for a kid after dark, even under the neon lights' cheery glow. Mercifully, Gregory has found himself an animatronic ally in the form of Freddy Fazbear. Here the *fun* really starts.

Wire-strewn backstage areas, box-filled basements, and sewers reveal the darker side to the Pizzaplex that cannot be unseen. This unlikely robo-partnership with Freddy gives Gregory access to main attractions, too, but mysterious nighttime protocols make for a wild ride . . .

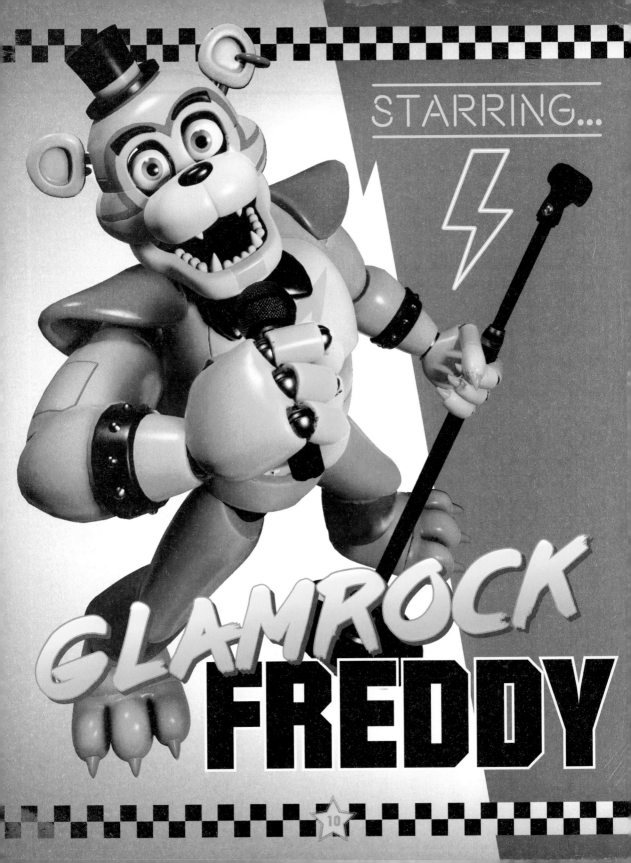

STARRING...

GLAMROCK FREDDY

During a spectacular stage show, "frontman" Freddy Fazbear collapses in front of the crowded arena! In some kind of system shock, Freddy later reboots in his Rockstar Row Green Room. Gregory, seeking a place to hide, has hitched a ride inside Freddy's belly compartment.

Freddy is only too happy to help Gregory, and fast becomes the ultimate personal assistant. The amazing Faz-Watch keeps the duo connected whenever Gregory needs to explore solo, that secret stomach area (usually reserved for piñatas and "oversized birthday cakes") keeps Gregory shielded from most Pizzaplex patrols. Part tour guide, part bodyguard, all buddy.

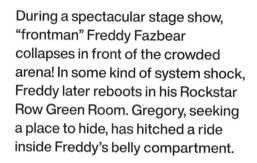

It would be too easy, though, for Gregory to rely on Freddy too much. There are limitations. Like, Freddy needs to recharge his batteries every once in a while, encouraging Gregory to go it alone. Owing to Freddy's bulk, he cannot sneak into smaller spaces like his pal. Freddy mostly advises via Faz-Watch and can be summoned to Gregory's side when possible.

Also, the way Gregory finds Freddy in the early hours of this "adventure" is not his final form. The kind and charismatic animatronic undergoes some major upgrades before the night is through. And, you know, they're hardly what you would call "off-the-shelf" parts.

MEET GREGORY

One of the biggest advantages of being a kid is that you're small. You're usually fast, too. Combine these traits with resourcefulness and youthful optimism, and you stand a chance. From the moment he springs from Freddy's belly, Gregory keeps it moving, thinking smart.

Sneaking, by crouching, is often the wisest strategy for Gregory, which reduces noise and lowers his profile. He is, however, much slower while being stealthy. In order to move while remaining completely unseen, Gregory sticks to the creepy corners and haunting shadows.

Another major attribute is meddling hands. Forget every time you've been told DO NOT TOUCH, because prying and poking stuff is highly recommended around the Pizzaplex. Abandoned duffel bags and prize boxes contain many key items, plus some cool collectibles. There are also noisemakers dotted around the venue such as old paint cans. Knocking these over creates a distraction.

Of course there are some scary circumstances when the only thing to do is RUN. Being a hero of the not-so-super variety, though, means that Gregory easily runs out of steam. His stamina bar indicates when it's time for a rest. Always a worry while being chased . . .

USE IT...
OR LOSE IT

Gregory learns fast how to survive, with the Faz-Watch as the centerpiece of all the items he needs. This Freddy souvenir connects the duo online and stores all intel discovered: emails from angry parents, staff memos, and more. It monitors security cams, provides a map, and keeps track of the latest missions. With Faz-Watch, Gregory has a chance to think before he acts.

1 FREE* PHOTO PASS!

Other early essentials include a Freddy Photo Pass, which is complimentary if you know where to look. This literally opens doors for Gregory, but higher levels of security require upgrades.

Not everything that Gregory needs is carried on his person. He soon learns to identify hiding spots, such as laundry carts, photo booths, and strollers. There are stacks of things that help create distractions: piles of paint cans being used for refurb or colorful playground toys.

Freddy often highlights the essentials, but Gregory is always on the lookout for anything conspicuous that might offer an advantage or secret reveal. Every location has something fun to interact with, or another part of the puzzle to trigger before leaving. You'd like to think that Gregory gets used to everything he touches having consequences.

IN THE HUNT

Freddy was the only animatronic to get fried during the concert. His Glamrock bandmates Chica, Roxanne "Roxy" Wolf, and Montgomery "Monty" Gator are all still primed to round up intruders and . . . who knows what they will do upon capturing. Inside the first hour, Gregory gets used to baiting these guys. The best he can do is keep the noise down and stay out of their way.

Chica Chicken

Montgomery Gator

Roxanne Wolf

Meanwhile, an apparently well-meaning security guard, Vanessa, is also "doing the rounds." Gregory doesn't much trust her, either. He learns to scan every wide-open area for signs of flash- light and movement in his peripheral vision— excellent training for challenges ahead.

Chica is the first major encounter in which Gregory must use his stealthy smarts to outwit; she'll give chase if not extra, extra careful. It's Monty who serves up the first major scare and hair-raisin' test of how useful Gregory is at running. Don't look back! (Or not for long.)

Just when you think the chase is over . . . it isn't over. That's kind of a theme going on.

12:00 a.m.

HARD RULES IN HARD PLAY

Glamrock Freddy takes time out to recharge, which leaves Gregory to find his way into the Pizzaplex. This lobby entrance (where Chica is also present) is a jaw-dropping sight, made to feel even more exclusive by its ticket holders–only turnstiles. The whole place feels like stepping into a 1980s mall.

Gregory plots his own route through this swanky, wide-open space, calculating many risks. Freddy makes it clear where Gregory *should* go, but there are so many more areas where Gregory *could* go to claim rewards. He can watch and wait for low-risk opportunities from his place in the shadows or check the security-cam feed on Faz-Watch. The tension slowly builds . . .

Even when Gregory follows simple instructions to his next destination, the path ahead is hardly ever straight. Main entrances are all gated and locked, leaving Gregory searching for other ways around. Once inside, things may not work as expected, but clues can be found.

"THIS AREA IS OFF-LIMITS."
═ CHICA ═

The Pizzaplex lobby is a training ground for Gregory, before the hunting party turns up the heat. It gets him used to thinking about all the up and down, front and back of the place—how not to get spotted in larger spaces, and how to navigate through tighter, claustrophobic ones.

FITNESS
through

FOOD

UNDER LOCK AND KEY

It's important to know that one thing, a lot of the time, leads to another in the Pizzaplex. A Complimentary Entry Pass only gets Gregory so far. A malfunctioning machine involves a modest little work-around quest, reminding him of low-level danger from security patrols.

GET A COMPLIMENTARY ENTRY PASS!

Some acquisitions are strictly temporary, and soon replaced. The security badge is needed many times to grant access, but its status requires upgrading several times. Some items trigger an event the moment Gregory has them in his grasp. Anything not neatly wrapped or tucked in a bag can spell trouble! That "what now?!" sinking sensation of dread becomes familiar fast.

REMEMBER TO VISIT...

Glamrock Gifts

One way to survive the night is to keep movement to a minimum, scurrying like a frightened mouse between hidey holes. Do only what's necessary, and easy on the nerves. C'mon, Gregory is made of steelier stuff than that. Take a good look around, explore in every direction, and this puny lost kid will find powerful secrets to bring his story to an ASTOUNDING conclusion.

Meanwhile, the most illuminating and essential item offered to Gregory just after midnight is the flashlight. Superstar Daycare is the first real test of navigation in near-total darkness.

CHICA
ON THE
PROWL

Chica has also joined the hunt. So, there's a couple of ways Chica ends up running after Gregory: The obvious one is her clapping eyes on the kid, which happens due to carelessness and can be avoided. Running the gauntlet of bots may be trickier because they shift so crazily in tight spaces.

In no time at all, Gregory and Freddy have stirred the hornet's nest. Pizzaplex security bots are activated, scooting swiftly around polished floors, armed with . . . flashlights? They might appear harmless, but should Gregory be caught, they raise the alarm, and that is very bad.

"HEY, HEY, ARE YA HAVING FUN YET? ARE YA?"
═ CHICA ═

It makes the habit of checking security-cam feeds that much more important. And, to do that, Gregory needs to make better use of hiding spots. All of which sharpens survival skill, and brings the thrill of gaining confidence. And Gregory hasn't much hope without this.

After outwitting the attendant in Superstar Daycare (more about that on the next page), the rest of the Glamrock animatronics triangulate Gregory's position. The chase is on, and to cap it all off, there's the first sighting of a dancing rabbit lady . . . or, at least Gregory sees this. It seems to pass Freddy clean on by.

DON'T ASK...
"WHY ANIMATRONICS?"

ASK INSTEAD...
"WHY NOT MORE ANIMATRONICS?"

CAUTION

WET FLOOR

SLIDE INTO FUN!

LUNAPHOBIA

Jettisoned into a ball pit from a tubular slide, Gregory is suddenly locked inside a primary-colored prison with the most eccentric roommate. No amount of joyful "music" can make Superstar Daycare anything less than disquieting. There's something eerie about a soft-play area with no visitors. Gregory must keep moving to avoid getting caught, and plan his escape.

SUPERSTAR DAYCARE PICK-UP
DAYCARE PASS REQUIRED FOR ENTRY

Initially, the room is brightly lit so that Gregory can get his bearings. Little does Gregory know, at this stage, that he will soon be stranded in the pitch-blackness, scrambling for safety among the railings of the jungle gym. Daycare is the first occasion when Gregory absolutely needs a plan of action to make clean work of the confusing task lying ahead.

Gregory triggers a power failure immediately upon collecting the Security Badge, which is waiting for him at the reception desk. With the lights gone, the only way out of daycare is by restoring power to five generators. Gregory is wise to plot their whereabouts in advance, to avoid marching blindly into the clutches of Moon, the attendant's nighttime alter ego.

A flashlight is found near the counter to pierce the darkness. Without orientation, however, Gregory is sentenced to always stumbling back into Moon's gleeful clutches . . .

THE KIDS ALL LOVE IT!

Superstar Daycare is the first, though by no means last, sighting of the terrifying two-faced attendant. Mocking in bright attire under artificial illumination as Sun. Prowling in mournful hues in the darkness as Moon. Whenever Pizzaplex lights power down, Moon resumes the hunt for Gregory and Freddy. It's one of the hardest-working animatronics around for sure.

To make Sun/Moon more appealing to the trusting little ones, the Pizzaplex publicity department has started marketing Sunnydrop Energizing Candy! and Moondrop Sleepy-Time Candy! Sun/Moon is the infant-friendly face of the place, with imagery festooned on so many walls.

What's not to trust?

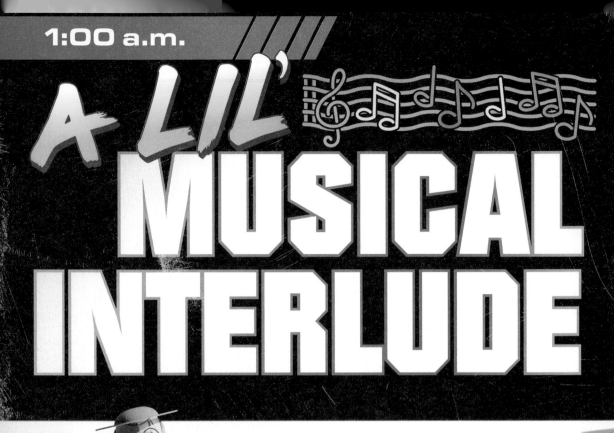

A LIL' MUSICAL INTERLUDE

Still haunted by his sighting of "dancing rabbit lady," but with Freddy confidently picking up the pace, Gregory is emboldened to make his choice of where next. There are two areas, just a short elevator ride down, accessed from the atrium: Loading Dock and Prize Counter.

Now, 1 a.m. is way past a sensible bedtime for a kid, but the enormity of Gregory's escape bid is enough to make anyone feel weary at the prospect. To help underline this point, a Map Bot hands over a Faz Map to browse on the Faz-Watch. Huge, complex areas run across many floors.

Both available routes introduce a vent-crawling entity, Lil' Music Man, as Gregory squeezes into the airducts toward the Loading Dock or Prize Counter. Whichever destination Gregory goes for, once Lil' Music Man gives chase, there is no going back. Something about a teeny, beat-up, grimacing animatronic makes you never want to turn around and face the music.

After surviving the trials of Loading Dock or Prize Counter, just as he sees himself as quite the escape artist, Gregory is finally rounded up by Vanessa, the security guard. Mysteriously, at some point during this encounter, Gregory is left unconscious. Maybe he was feeling tired . . .

THE LOADING DOCK

These are places that regular Pizzaplex customers (those that are not locked in after hours) never get to see or know about. As Gregory's journey reveals more about the mega venue, he's also handed more decision-making opportunities. These include flashlight management—fear of the dark vs. battery life. Flashlight upgrades can be found, but only by those brave and industrious enough to seek them out. This is all about gaining confidence and fighting back.

TAKE WHAT'S YOURS...
ROXIE COLA
LIMITED EDITION FIZZYFAZ

FIZZYFAZ

Amid the Fizzyfaz syrup vats, Gregory becomes the prowler while Chica is on the march. Little does the lead-guitar animatronic suspect that she will be played like an old record in the minutes to come. Between them, Freddy and Gregory concoct quite the delicious plan.

SODARONI
A SIGNATURE PEPPERONI FLAVOR

However, as the tactics improve from Freddy and Gregory, the S.T.A.F.F. presence increases, with mop bots joining the security patrol. Better timing, combined with daredevil intuition, is needed to navigate laundry rooms bustling with these servo-driven Pizzaplex servants.

The stakes have been raised; the response must be strong. Successfully navigating this route guides Gregory inevitably into the clutches of Vanessa, but now he's in command of hiding spots, Faz-Cam feeds, and well-timed roadie runs to safety. There are four more hours to survive.

PIZZA X-PRESS!

In this time of need, it is time to feed. It turns out Chica is one ravenous animatronic. All it takes to keep her busy is "the perfect mouthwatering pizza." Trapped in the Kitchen Office, Gregory logs into Freddy Fazbear's Mega Pizzaplex quick-delivery virtual ordering system.

SAUCE

CHEESE

MEAT

NOT MEAT

PIZZA

As with everything else so far, the next steps are not nearly as straightforward as expected. There's no delivery to the door. Gregory goes against the clock to prepare and bake this life-saving pie, remote-controlling a pizza-making S.T.A.F.F. bot. As Gregory comes to grips with the pizzabot, adding sauce, cheese, delicious meat, and "not meat" stuff, Chica is pounding on the door.

Until now, time pressure has been self-imposed. This crash course in pizzabot management, anxiously waiting on the oven to perform the final task, makes for heart-in-mouth moments. Door integrity decreasing by the second is intimidating. But after Gregory has conquered this episode, having gratified the Glamrock glutton, he draws closer to being indestructible.

In the closing moments of the Loading Dock encounter, tension placed temporarily "on ice," Freddy introduces another element of doubt to trouble Gregory's mind. Just when the kid thought he'd cleared the way, the security level is raised way higher than it should be.

As with the alternate Loading Dock route, an army of mop bots present problems for Gregory in the Pizzaplex East Arcade. Roxy is hunting close by, meaning that collisions with security or mopping S.T.A.F.F. could result in Gregory being captured. Handily, it is super dark, and the many machines make it easy to break line of sight with the self-obsessed animatronic.

ROCKING WITH ...

ROXANNE WOLF

Passing through El Chip's restaurant, Gregory can collect a Fizzyfaz stamina upgrade that, similar to flashlight upgrades, primes him for later ordeals. Sprinting longer, putting distance between Gregory and his pursuers, is handy to do early. There are four flavors to collect. Each flavor represents a member of the Glamrock band, and each one energizes with a stamina boost.

With conventional exits blocked off from the East Arcade, Gregory slides into the Pizzaplex vents where he is chased by Lil' Music Man. It's the kind of thing that any sensible young human instinctively runs away from, and Gregory does so, passing a point of no return.

"YOU CAN'T HIDE FOREVER."
ROXY

The vent dumps Gregory like a sack of potatoes into the Prize Counter Security Office, where a Security Level 2 badge is offered. Taking it is a trap, which triggers a lockdown, summoning Monty and Roxy. Just how good are Gregory's security-cam skills? He is about to find out.

PRIZE COUNTER
THIS WAY!

FAZBEAR ENTERTAINMENT IS **NOT** RESPONSIBLE FOR THEFT OR LOSS OF ITEMS OR INJURY

If Gregory has been relying a whole lot on his own eyes and ears to evade danger until this point, the next three minutes can be a mountain to climb. Cameras are placed to give views of all corridors and exits close to the Security Office. The office is really super tiny, with not much space to hide. Monty and Roxy are almost certain to spy Gregory from either doorway without effort. Gregory could pick a spot, close his eyes, rely on luck, but if all goes wrong . . .

Better to do things properly—consider it further training—and master flicking between cam feeds, shutting doors briefly to preserve their power. These three minutes can feel like 300 hours in a state of panic, but keeping things calm really is key to locking the bad guys out. When the lockdown ends, Monty and Roxy slouch disgruntledly toward the Prize Counter.

Natural hide-and-seek skills are enough to see Gregory make his escape via the Prize Counter elevator, as long as he keeps checking corners, marine style. Within the Prize Counter area, a huge glass-domed feature allows Gregory to spy on Roxy without her knowing. She's not smart enough to use such tactics herself, which is sooo helpful.

But as brilliant as this escape bid surely is, all the activity caught the attention of Vanessa, who apprehends Gregory just as soon as he enters the elevator. Such a crushing blow!

DANCING RABBIT LADY SAYS HI!

Screwdriver

We find Gregory staring a GAME OVER situation square in its face, and it is over fast unless he's quick to act. Locked in Lost and Found, Gregory is told that the only way out is in the company of his parents, or the police. Vanessa's scowling face fills the office monitors.

Bad enough, but the scenario takes an even darker turn with the distorted visage of Vanny (aka "dancing rabbit lady") replacing Vanessa. Luckily this is soon fixed with a simple screwdriver, used to pry open an air vent to escape!

With Vanny's dismembered voice whispering in his ears, Gregory takes flight to the Atrium elevator. It's here where Freddy regains contact but is heard struggling to maintain it, due to "something" jamming his comms. Everything is happening so fast now. Gregory is directed to the Roxy Raceway, indicated on the Atrium map. It's easy to find, but S.T.A.F.F. bots are out in force, harassing Gregory while he searches for a blocked route that Freddy mentioned.

When Gregory is finally reunited with Freddy, his powerful animatronic guardian is lying helpless on the floor. He needs access to Parts and Service, but before that he enters Rest Mode while Gregory heads off to the Glamrockers' inner sanctum. Let's go backstage!

ACCESS ALL AREAS

The area beneath the main stage is messy beyond belief. Great, because there is plenty to explore. Bothersome, since corridors have keen-lensed security bots whizzing up and down, forcing Gregory into side rooms, or frozen in shadows between dim pools of essential light.

Roxy is listening for any sign of activity from her S.T.A.F.F. bot assistants, too, and is fast to respond. The urge is to rush to save Freddy; however, it is wisest to watch and wait for the cleanest opportunities in such a narrow space. It sure is a dramatic contrast to the Atrium.

SAFETY GUIDELINES
FOR OPERATING FORKLIFTS

- ONLY USE FOR BOXES AT/ABOVE 100LBS
- NO FORKLIFT RACES
- NEVER ELEVATE ANIMATRONICS
- KEEP FORKLIFTS OUT OF WALKWAYS
- PAY ATTENTION WHILE DRIVING
- REMEMBER TO USE BRAKES
- FORKLIFTS OFF LIMITS DURING BUSINESS HOURS

"YOU ARE NOTHING." — ROXY

Locating a Backstage Pass in the Rehearsal Room is a breeze by comparison; it's cozy and quiet. Gregory has all the time he needs . . . and b-r-e-a-t-h-e. It's a short hop round the corner now, back to Rockstar Row. Here the pass grants access to Stage Controls: Staff Only.

Gregory is becoming the master of the Pizzaplex, thanks to Freddy's help. It is now time for Gregory to return the favor, helping his depleted buddy secure a long overdue recharge. Almost halfway through this troubled night, the crazy levels are due to rise another notch.

SCREAM TIME

Does anything about this look familiar to you? Hmmm . . .

Another trap is triggered in the Stage Controls room, immediately after Gregory acquires his Security Level 3 badge. Along with it, an old peculiar performance disk, and, somehow in between, Gregory has fixed Freddy's problematic signal. No time to party, though! Monty and Roxy commence hammering on the doors. Vanny is racing Freddy to an area located beneath the floor. Decades from now, when he is an old dude, Gregory may remember this day fondly!

There's enough juice to power five sets of doors for Freddy to duck into and reach Gregory. Smaller units of power are burned when smashing buttons that shock animatronics behind the Controls room doors. This is a set-piece showdown, keeping Gregory constantly moving, listening out for Freddy's cries of "over here!" Every door opened drains a whopping chunk. If the doors to the room run out of power completely, Monty and Roxy can rush right in.

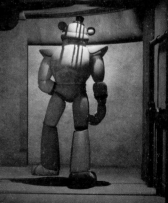

By keeping this going (without too many mistakes), Gregory is returned to his Glamrock robot-pal, reaching up through a vent beneath the Controls room. You've got this, Gregory!

STAGE FRIGHT

Since you asked, that old disk is a Program Disk, used to activate the Glamrock stage show. Freddy knows just the place to take it. On this occasion, though he is very grateful, he won't be chauffeuring Gregory in his belly; until they reach Parts and Service, he's low on power.

The guys return to the Atrium, by way of a winding underground passage leading directly to the stage. On any other occasion, there would be crowds of Freddy Fazbear fans going wild. Tonight, the Pizzaplex sees Roxy and Chica pacing levels two and three while Monty shines a spotlight from high above the show floor. They have been waiting for the show to start.

Putting into practice everything he has learned since 11 p.m., Gregory winds his way upward to the Sound Booth. Occasionally, he steps into a photo booth to check the cam feed for signs of roaming animatronics, gets his bearings in relation to the Sound Booth, and times the gaps between security bot traffic just right. A lot of crouching, and tactical use of stamina.

On his way back down, Gregory is panicked to find Monty joining Roxy on the ground floor. Vanny is also somewhere around, indicated by a mysterious mind-numbing haze. Keeping the stage area in sight, measuring steps between the dining tables, Gregory makes it back.

NIGHT, NIGHT FREDDY

At last! Freddy and Gregory together again! They're maybe one Recharge Station away from blowing this joint. Gregory strikes the button that activates the lift to Parts and Service.

With the hour almost up, approaching 3 a.m., Gregory remembers the "moon thing" from Superstar Daycare. Right on cue, Moon is spied taunting the friends from the edge of the platform . . . almost certainly waiting for them below. Keeping it simple, Freddy suggests heading straight for the Recharge Station, and fast. It's dark and disorienting down there. Moon reminds Gregory that it's past bedtime, spooking him under the flashlight beam.

This is all a distraction to strike fear into Gregory, who makes a run for the Recharge Station as instructed. The door hisses shut. Outside, Moon is dragging Freddy's lifeless body away.

It's about to get worse.

PARTS AND SERVICE

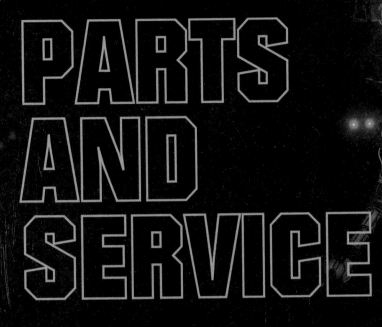

Shortly into the fifth hour of this mess, Gregory faces another dilemma in the form of Endos. These are the skeletal insides of animatronics, with a particularly alarming habit: They only move to attack whenever their target's back is turned. Nobody, not even Freddy, thinks to tell this to Gregory. He learns the hard way, using observation combined with instinct.

Just one Endo is tricky to deal with when you're still balancing flashlight power, stamina, and general navigation skills. Consider, then, the task of outmaneuvering multiple Endos! Gregory needs to be in full control of his current capabilities, all while stepping backward. Also, he needs to know what's behind him while moving backward, in case of *more Endos*.

So basics, like button-pressing; Gregory has a limited time window to do this with an Endo on his tail. Keeping Endos a good distance away is important. Using the flashlight to recon a room, not simply for comfort, is important—Gregory saves battery life for when he needs it.

The ultimate Endo encounter in this hour involves Gregory attempting to retrieve his badge for Security Level 4. Inside the Security Office are a bunch of inactive Endos, literally just hanging. As soon as the badge is snatched, the Endos power up to engage the perpetrator. Everything about Gregory's approach needs to be considered to avoid being surrounded.

KEEPING IT MOVING

Gregory's first mission in Parts and Service is to reach the Warehouse Security Office, which is a lot easier said than done. The Warehouse is security-gated lengths of corridor sectioned off behind movable walls. Having just completed an ad hoc Endo tutorial at the entrance, Gregory is prepared for similar encounters to come. But there's another layer of the puzzle.

To progress through the mazelike network of tunnels, Gregory must press a button to move the nearby wall. Each time Gregory does this, the Endos in his current zone are all activated. The lesson to learn here is that the way back is treacherous, and only return fully prepared.

BE CAREFUL

100% OF FATAL ACCIDENTS INVOLVE HUMAN BEINGS

Just knowing that the Endos are patrolling the exit route, while Gregory is otherwise simply retracing his steps, is paralyzing. The return leg of the Warehouse sequence calls upon all Gregory's guile when using hiding spots (Parts and Service carts), and his sense of direction.

The punch line to the Warehouse setup is that Gregory can quite easily make headway into the maze, without too much caution, as long as he keeps moving.

PICKING UP THE PIECES

A few things Gregory gets to hear are not intended for his ears, which is something worth remembering. Like, the conversation between Vanessa and Freddy at the beginning of the Parts and Service mission. Anyway, Gregory next finds Freddy in some kind of maintenance suite, sorely in need of repair. Like, badly in need of a head on his shoulders.

To "reconnect the wires," Gregory matches his wits against a color-coded memory game to match rapid-fire sequences. Once to perform this operation, and again to run diagnostics. If Gregory gets this wrong, he is reminded of the potential dangers of trusting animatronics.

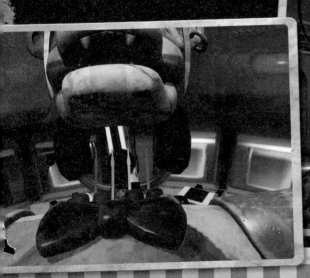

Before going ahead with the procedure, a nearby console shows Gregory some of the other possibilities for Freddy, much further down the line. Power, Claws, Voicebox, and Ocular are listed. Gregory learns that Chica, Roxy, and Monty have all benefited from such upgrades. Would Freddy consider such things? It's an ethical issue that Freddy finds hard to deal with.

There's no need for any of this just now, though. Freddy, back on his feet and feeling much better, has more survival tips for Gregory. He sure needs them for what's up next . . .

Select Upgrade

▶ Power Upgrade
Claws Upgrade
Voicebox Upgrade
Ocular Upgrade
Exit

THE RIGHT TO PARTY

Next stop, Chica's Green Room in Rockstar Row! There, Gregory hopes to bag a Party Pass, with the long-term plan of acquiring gizmos to halt bothersome bots in their tracks. This is Gregory showing some strategizing powers of his own, thinking about how to make life easier.

See, both Fazer Blast and Monty Golf attractions require a Party Pass for entry. There are the Fazerblaster and Faz-Cam, respectively, to fetch from these attractions. These devices will confuse bots long enough to create distance. Bots don't like bright lights in the eyes. Take it from Freddy.

During this episode, the secretive "backstage" thrill is so real as Gregory takes the service elevator (the only one that works) to Roxy's Green Room. It's better for Freddy to smuggle the kid through the keyboard player's trashed boudoir, so as not to upset her any further.

The route to Chica's Green Room is complex enough to make the Party Pass feel like the prize it oughta be—another zip through the vents with Lil' Music Man clattering behind. Remember the Screwdriver from earlier? It saves Gregory's skin, yet again. Go tools!

C'mon, every fan's dream is to hang out in the Green Room of their favorite rock star . . . even better if they're a Glamrock animatronic! When they're not kicking back (or being serviced), here's where the gang rehearses moves and licks, getting amped before lighting up the stage.

THE GREEN ROOMS

GOOD NIGHT!
SEE YA NEXT TIME

Yet more of the Pizzaplex is now open to Gregory, thanks to the Party Pass, which he simply shows a party bot to enter. This definition of Party, though, is not in any dictionary we know.

No sooner is the Party Pass in Gregory's pocket than scary "moon thing" miasma descends. If Gregory has been following his own code of conduct, being a super-inquisitive kid first of all, he is aware of a backroom Recharge Station, safe haven from Moon, to survive the hour. In case Gregory is still getting by, bumbling around, it may take Freddy's advice to go looking for Recharge Stations, which, by the way, are highlighted right there on the Faz-Watch map.

Party Pass

"IT'S PAST YOUR BEDTIME."
— MOONDROP

PARTY TIME!

So Party Pass is a one-time-only ticket, which means that Gregory's next couple hours will be defined by his choice of either Monty Golf or Fazer Blast. To get this party started, Gregory roves the Pizzaplex one last time before fully committing to the chain of events that follow.

By now, Gregory has survived countless jump scares while solving a few mysteries. He's used to searching high and low for duffel bags and prize boxes, has a knack for side-stepping S.T.A.F.F. bots, and is unfazed if he accidentally raises any alarms. Gregory's Pizzaplex survival skills might have plateaued; however, there is still a mountain to climb before reaching the climax.

As dawn approaches, Gregory will be considerably better armed and dangerous. Bots won't know what hit them. Freddy will receive literally game-changing upgrades, turning the tide.

Between 4 a.m. to 5 a.m., Gregory and Freddy are spectacularly transformed. Whether choosing Fazer Blast or Monty Golf first, the opportunity to return and finish both jobs is irresistible. Rewards for doing so are extremely worthwhile. They need to be. This is the final countdown.

HERE
COMES ...

MONTGOMERY
GATOR

62

As much as Gregory would love a round of Gator Golf, there are wilder games afoot tonight. Using his Party Pass to gain entry here is purely to reach the back office, which has a huge stash of items to plunder. Thankfully, the Monty roars are for atmosphere only here.

Inside the office, Gregory finds an upgraded Security Badge, Faz Camera, and a ticket for the Mazercise attraction on Level 3. For now, the Faz Camera is the biggest win, since it can stun groups of S.T.A.F.F. bots and animatronics. All except Monty, because he's wearing shades!

Thus armed, and feeling ever more confident, Gregory exits Gator Golf and makes a beeline for Mazercise. For sure, somebody—or some*thing*—is messing with him, since Freddy soon realizes they need a Mazercise Control Key to make further progress. Gregory speeds past camera-equipped bots and Endos to the Fazbear Theater and grabs this key from the Wardrobe area.

GATOR GOLF!

D?
YOURSELF!

↑ 1 2 3 4 5
→ ↓

wait for help.
ter.

Different Maze
EVERY
HOUR!

This nerve-racking runaround eventually allows Gregory to manipulate some partitions in Mazercise to reveal a secret vent. He emerges in a cavernous room, where Monty himself is waiting to pounce.

In this Boss Battle, Gregory's expert aim allows him to hit plastic cannonballs into buckets. The cannons only have limited ammo, and Monty seeks to destroy them, but Gregory prevails by shooting balls into the largest bucket, then hitting a switch for the balls to land onto Monty and cause him to fall into a pit.

Gregory descends and helps himself to Monty's Claws from his enemy's shattered remains. The Monty upgrade allows Freddy to break gates and gain access to secret areas.

Sorry, NO AUTOGRAPHS

Monty needs to rest up for the next show!

"No running, no climbing, no jumping, no hitting, kicking, pushing, shoving. No shooting Fazerblasters close to players' eyes." Got to love Rule Number One of Fazer Blast, delivered flatly by an Instruction bot. Tonight, Fazer Blast is empty anyway. Gregory fights for Team Orange . . . alone. The buildup is awesome, with adrenaline rising as Gregory reaches for the Fazerblaster.

Inside Fazer Blast, the Alien Bots fall prey to Gregory's sharp-shooting smarts from playing video games. It's Capture the Flag, kinda, with zones to claim and protect. Directing the Alien Bots into Gregory's sights and camping behind cover count among perfectly viable tactics.

Bonnie BOWL

Victory earns Gregory a golden Fazerblaster to call his own, and straightaway to ignore Rule Number One when targeting bots and animatronics. As with Faz Camera, the Fazerblaster stuns its victims, all except Monty that is. The prize is waiting for Gregory in the VIP Room, where a vent also leads to Vanny's secret lair! You know, it always, always pays to explore.

Before leaving Fazer Blast, Gregory grabs a Security Badge and Bonnie Bowl Unlimited Pass from the office. The latter is needed to defeat Chica. See, behind the concessions counter at Bonnie Bowl, there is an office. In that office is a massive box of Monty Mystery Mix, which Gregory can use to his advantage with Chica. Together with Freddy, Gregory heads back to the Atrium food courts . . .

Monty Mystery Mix

TRASH COMPACTOR

TRASH TALK

With his new security clearance, Gregory takes the elevator down into the Kitchen where Chica was seen munching freshly made pizza. Inside the Kitchen there is a trash compactor, which Gregory sees as the perfect trap and places the Monty Mystery Mix inside.

Gregory powers up the machine and waits. Chica takes the bait and is instantly crushed! The result, apart from being not too pretty, is that Chica's Beak is yanked from its owner. Anyone would think this marks the end of Chica, but no! The battle continues in the Sewer, when Chica drags Gregory down with her.

CHICA'S BEAK

Chica's Beak helps Gregory through the metal door to the Sewer, where he is reacquainted with Shattered Chica. Using the Fazerblaster to keep her at bay, Gregory activates a series of generators to unlock related doors. It's tense, but after the third door, Gregory has a chance to escape and make his way back to the surface . . . pursued temporarily by Vanny!

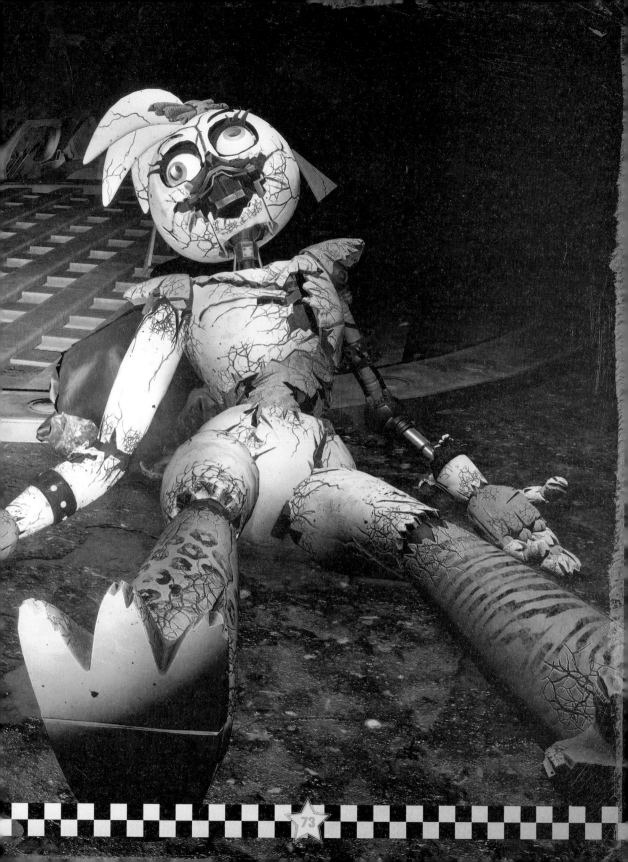

UPGRADING FREDDY

Once Gregory claims the animatronic parts, he hurries excitedly back to the upgrade station in Parts and Service. The color-coded sequences are much harder than they were when reattaching Freddy's head. For Chica's voice box, the operation involves peering into Freddy's chest cavity. To attach Monty's claws, Gregory must first remove part of Freddy's forearm. This upgrade is for either the voice box or the claws, you can only have one of these at this point . . .

Select Upgrade

Power Upgrade
Claws Upgrade
► **Voicebox Upgrade**
Ocular Upgrade
Exit

Upgraded Freddy is marvelous, though! With Chica's voicebox, he can stun animatronics. Monty's Claws slice clean through chains and access all those areas marked "No Monty." Great! That's two down! Now, where might that rascal Roxy have gone . . .?

START YOUR ENGINES!

Faced with a locked gate at the entrance to Roxy's Raceway, Gregory will have either Chica's Voice or Monty's Claws to work his way inside. It depends on the choice he made at 4 a.m., to target Monty or Chica. The one he chose to ignore is still roaming free around 5 a.m. Noooo!

HARD HAT AREA

ROXY RACEWAY

DON'T LOSE YOUR HEAD

The obvious thing to do at a raceway is find something to race with. But wait, the only available Racekart is missing a head for its driver! A lengthy search of Roxy's Raceway eventually leads to a broken S.T.A.F.F. bot, whose head looks about right for the job. Claiming this, Gregory seeks to repair it ASAP. Freddy tells Gregory there is a repair station at the West Arcade.

"SIGN UP TODAY AND BE A WINNER! NOBODY LIKES A LOSER."

— ROXY —

In order to reach the Maintenance Hall, Gregory first swings by the garages beneath Roxy's Raceway, where he finds a Dance Pass. After flashing this to the Party Bot at the entrance to the West Arcade, Gregory makes his way to the West Arcade Security Office. Unfortunately, the power goes down, sending Gregory on one of the most intense exercises of the night.

FAZCADE

As Gregory attempts to reboot the West Arcade, he is pursued by either Chica or Monty. The one he didn't already "decommission." If this is Monty, Gregory is in for a wild time!

Either way, the task itself here is straightforward (never say "easy"): Flip breaker switches, what could possibly go wrong? The first is easy to stumble upon, being right next to the DJ Music Man dance floor. The other switches . . . not so simple.

Two of the switches are on Level 1, where Monty enjoys launching at Gregory, closing the distance in the blink of an eye. On Level 2, Chica is prowling, where at least she can be stunned. Whichever predicament Gregory now finds himself in, he has nobody to blame but himself.

The final switch, found in the Maintenance Hall, summons the magnificent DJ Music Man. He gives chase, hurling junk at Gregory as our unlikely hero flees as fast as he can, testing his stamina to the limit. Pumped, Gregory returns to the Security Office to repair the robot head, and avail himself of the Level 7 Security Badge. Now, where were we? Yes, Roxy!

Head Deposit

Roxy's attempt to jump scare the Racekart equipped with the S.T.A.F.F. robot head spectacularly backfires. The tiny but super-heavy vehicle spirals out of control. It strikes Roxy square across the face, before pinning her to the floor. This particular battle is over, but the chase certainly is not. Gregory turns to flee.

WHERE'D YOU GET THOSE *EYES?*

After Gregory plucks the eyeballs from Roxy's shattered head, the animatronic soon returns in a berserker rage! While Gregory attempts to leave via a fragile wooden door, Roxy rams right through it. She continues like this, smashing more doors in blind pursuit of Gregory.

Using all tactics imaginable to draw Roxy's attention, including knocking over stacks of paint cans, Gregory reaches a vent at the far end of the final room. The night is almost at an end. Is there anything Gregory might've missed? Well, time to upgrade Freddy with Roxy's eyes.

GET OUT!

Freddy's Ocular Upgrade, one final multi-colored memory game, coincides with the dying minutes of the hour. Which means one thing: Moon from Daycare, hunting Gregory down.

This is Gregory's chance to escape, for real this time. Choosing the fastest route to the Main Lobby exit, Moon taunting him the whole way, a big decision awaits at the doors. Freddy is unable to leave. Will Gregory choose to stay? If yes, Gregory heads for "home sweet home." If no, Gregory can investigate further to stop Vanny . . .

Select Upgrade

Power Upgrade
Claws Upgrade
Voicebox
Upgrade
▶ Ocular
Upgrade
Exit

ESCAPE THE PIZZAPLEX!

Ending #1: Stay or Go?

Outside, birds are singing, and the sounds of freeway traffic are filtering through the Pizzaplex as delivery trucks lead the morning charge. Outside, Gregory can be free of this nightmare. Or . . . he can stay! And—with Freddy—fight to bring an end to these, umm, quite frankly terrible goings-on when the lights go down.

Immediately after Freddy's Ocular Upgrade, following Roxy's *spectacular* defeat, the Moon Man makes his final bid to capture Gregory. By far the easiest, safest, commonsense move to make is for Gregory to get the heck out and head home as fast as his legs can carry him. This, he can do, and with Freddy's approval and obvious gratitude, from the main entrance.

Sure, there is the matter of the Moon man to consider, but this isn't Gregory's first rodeo, and he has become a pro at evading him by now. Gregory escapes, only to end up living on the street . . . and Vanny finding him again.

COME BACK SOON!

If all Gregory wants to do is up and leave, there's also the option of the Loading Dock, accessed via the Kitchen area Salads & Sides, to make a swift exit. He'll need a Level 7 security clearance to take advantage of this, though the effort required to escape from here is worth it . . .

Main Entrance or Loading Dock, Gregory can quit. But, they call that . . . erm, quitting.

Of all the encounters Gregory faces, the specter of Vanny might forever haunt him were he to flee without some kind of closure. Well, such information is available. But only if Gregory has been enough of a sleuth to sniff out Vanny's secret hideout first. Chances are he shimmied upon this tucked-away area while pursuing Chica via Fazer Blast. However, in case Gregory saw Monty as an easy target at 1 a.m. instead, he'll need to explore quite a bit more for this.

See, choosing to stay at the Pizzaplex is not only brave but the absolute best thing to do if Gregory wants to try everything (breaking more rules) before never going back there again!

By remaining in the Pizzaplex, Gregory receives a shiny new Party Pass, granting access to any missed attractions. If he is yet to visit Fazer Blast, now is the time to do it. That rabbit lady's mysterious lair is accessed via the vents from the Fazer Blast office. Yeah, it's spooky.

Assuming all is good, Gregory has an additional choice along staying and leaving, flagged simply "Vanny." In case Gregory's nerves are not already fried enough, this doesn't bode well for Freddy, and leads to a hair-raising chase to a distant exit. That Fazerblaster sure comes in handy!

DISASSEMBLE VANNY!

GREGORY...

Exploring. It's awesome. You should definitely try it. Here's another great reason why it makes fabulous sense for Gregory. In true 1980s style, there are three playable arcade cabinets called *Princess Quest* in the Pizzaplex. The first two are kinda hidden away.

Gregory, unable to resist checking every dark and dusty corner, is sure to have discovered the first one, located in the Famous Glamrock Beauty Salon. It's off the beaten track, next to Roxy's Raceway. The second *Princess Quest* coin-op is where Gregory raced like never before to flee DJ Music Man, in the shady extremities of the West Arcade, aka Fazcade.

To play the final cabinet, Gregory simply chooses to pursue Vanny at whichever exit he chooses, where he is then rushed to Vanny's secret hideaway. Inside is the *Princess Quest* machine. Now, it could be that Gregory is a newbie when it comes to 1980s arcade-style video games. In which case, completing *Princess Quest* could be harder than it looks.

Again, the ending isn't in Freddy's absolute best interests. But it is definitely better than the basic ending. Although, nothing could be much worse than that. Only here to state the facts.

Once Gregory has tempered his nerves of steel, all that animatronic avoidance a mere trifle, the Pizzaplex is a fun place to be. No, truly! In fact, Gregory can even take time out to smell the fake flowers and point his handy Faz Camera at random (or is it?) stuff left lying around.

Golden Sun

Six such treasures, Golden Plushies, are found in gilded prize boxes, though in places where Gregory needs to be especially inventive to access. There are also four character cutouts—Bonnie, Chica, Freddy, and Foxy—to enshrine as instant photos before the Golden Moon plushie can be unlocked. To shoot them all, visit the Daycare Theater basement, Kid's Cove, the West Arcade, and the area behind Rockstar Row.

After photographing them all, Gregory can enter a hidden door behind the Captain Foxy's Pirate Adventure poster in the Fazbear Theater to access the final plushie and a secret Balloon Boy arcade minigame. Gregory needs to move fast, though, to reach the VIP exit at the Prize Counter before getting himself caught. Revelations that follow are LEGENDARY.

And yet, even this cannot prepare Gregory for the grand finale. And that, Freddy Fazbear family, is rewarded for becoming, beyond doubt, every animatronic's worst nightmare.

Ending #6: BURN IT ALL DOWN

For this ending, you have to use both Monty's and Chica's abilities and get to the elevator shaft hidden next to the Fazer Blast exit.

Taking this elevator leads to the charred remnants of Freddy Fazbear's Pizza Place from Five Nights at Freddy's Pizzeria Simulator. Once there, Gregory encounters The Blob, a grotesque combination of cables and pieces of other animatronics. Gregory eventually ends up in a secret office where he faces off with Burntrap—a Withered Spring Bonnie animatronic merged with the body of Five Nights at Freddy's antagonist William Afton. Defeat Afton, and this ending is yours.

Ruin is free additional downloadable content for *Security Breach*—a whole new story set in the same location, after the events of the main game. The Pizzaplex lies derelict after an earthquake—and somewhere inside it, Gregory is trapped . . .

Five Nights at Freddy's

SECURITY BREACH

RUIN

MEET CASSIE

Cassie is a huge fan of the Fazbear franchise—her father was a maintenance worker for Fazbear Entertainment. She met Gregory at her birthday party, which her friends didn't show up to, and they became best friends. Cassie's nervous, but she pushes through it as she tries to find and rescue Gregory. But is this all a trap?

TOOLS

FLASHLIGHT

An essential accessory for exploring any derelict entertainment complex! Cassie didn't bring one with her, but she finds one in the hand of a security bot slumped in a booth in the lobby.

ROXY-TALKIE

This allows Cassie to communicate with Gregory, and he offers her guidance. Gregory talks to her using his Glamrock Freddy-Talkie.

WRENCH

This allows Cassie to complete the circuit puzzles that crop up regularly. In all these, the wires can be charged up but will start to go down when the wrench is removed. The trick is to get the power in every wire into the blue zone at once, switching the Faz-Wrench between the wires.

SECURITY MASK

It's Vanny's mask from the main game, and it brings Cassie into the cyberspace AR world, where she can make repairs to security nodes, operate special AR cameras, and walk through spaces that were previously obstructed! It's all good! Well, except it leaves Cassie vulnerable to attacks from the Entity, a virus that infects AR. Whenever Cassie wears the Security Mask, the Entity moves gradually toward her and, if he reaches her, summons an animatronic to attack. This means Cassie must work quickly when doing puzzles in AR. The mask also allows her to communicate with HELPY and see collectibles that aren't visible in the real world.

WALK-THROUGH

>>> ENTRANCE

Cassie makes her way into the Pizzaplex through a broken window, then drops into the mall and down a ladder to the lobby. A gateway leads to a darker area, and Cassie needs to light it up by getting the flashlight from the security bot.

Cassie makes her way upstairs, where she hears Gregory's voice, pleading for help! When she tracks down the source of the noise, it's actually a discarded Roxy-Talkie, which Gregory speaks through, telling Cassie he's been captured and is in the sinkhole underneath Roxy's Raceway.

Cassie heads off to help, going through the open elevator doors and taking the ladder up the elevator shaft. At the top of the shaft is an area where Cassie can crawl through a vent, which collapses as she's making her way around, sending her tumbling into the kitchen! We're starting to feel like this place might not be safe . . .

Going through the kitchen, which is full of disgusting, rotting food, Cassie runs into Chica, who jump-scares her but then deactivates. Cassie proceeds and picks up the Faz-Wrench— "Just like my dad's"—from a toolbox and uses it to tackle the first of several circuit puzzles.

>>> Fill the lower one first, then move to the upper one to complete the puzzle. Cassie continues onward through maintenance corridors until she reaches a pipe—and when she looks into it, Monty Gator attacks . . .

>>> MONTY'S GATOR GOLF

After running from Monty, Cassie finds herself in the derelict golf course, crouching down to get through. At the end, she runs into Map Bot, who gives Cassie the Security Mask, which she uses to get through the blocked door. Cassie finds another Faz-Wrench panel, which she can fix by fully charging the upper cable, then moving to the lower cable. Going through the bathroom, she finds a locked door that she can "open" by putting on the Security Mask.

As Cassie proceeds, she finds a Fazbear Technician Remote Camera Station, with which she can access the security cameras and locate Monty. Using the intercom, she can draw Monty toward a camera, distracting him to clear her route. Cassie can play the arcade game if she likes—it offers nine holes of Fazbear-themed golf. When she arrives at the fence, Monty briefly appears again.

When Cassie follows Monty, Gregory tells her she has to shut down all security measures. Using the Security Mask, she can get through the blocked stairway and the obstruction on the walkway. There she finds a mother node—a floating hologram of a bunny head. Cassie can deactivate its child node by following the glowing red wire coming from the base of the hologram. It's very close by and is in the form of a barrel.

>>> Interacting with the child node unlocks the mother node, which brings up a simple puzzle. This activates the forklift, which Cassie ducks under. After crawling through a tunnel made of boxes, she can use her Security Mask to find another mother node. This one has two wires leading to child nodes: a cutout of Monty's face and a toxic barrel. Deactivating one triggers the first appearance of the Entity . . .

WALK-THROUGH

>>> MONTY'S GATOR GOLF

The Entity will summon Monty if he reaches Cassie, so she should remove the mask whenever possible. A shutter rises after completing the mother node puzzle, leading to *another* mother node. The three child nodes are a red trash can, a golf club, and a plushie on a shelf. When Cassie heads back to the door, Monty appears and causes a tunnel to collapse, which opens a new route.

Another Faz-Wrench puzzle awaits Cassie at the end of this path. It needs to have the lower cable filled first, then the upper cable. This unlocks a door that leads to another mother node: The child nodes are a ball and a pizza. When Cassie completes the puzzle, the Entity appears—so she must remove the mask immediately.

Farther along, Cassie finds another mother node—it's better to get the child node on the upper floor first (it's a small box behind a chair, on the same level as the mother node). The Entity will appear after it's triggered, and Cassie can avoid him by heading down immediately. The other child node is a plushie on a conveyor on a lower level, and Cassie can remove the mask before going back to the mother node.

>>> The next area is a camera station, and if Cassie puts on the Security Mask, she can use it to see and quarantine anomalies. Destroying the Monty cutout in AR will create a path in the real world, which means Cassie can escape into Daycare . . .

WALK-THROUGH

>>> DAYCARE

Gregory informs Cassie she needs to head for the Daycare Theater. First, she needs to go through the playpen, which she can reach by going past the arcade machines, up the boxes, and down the slide. As she proceeds through the soft play area, Moon grabs her—but the flashlight scares him away.

After using the mask to get through a blockage, Cassie meets Sun, who wants her to use the Faz-Wrench to reboot him and tells her to turn the generators on to activate the lights. After this, he doesn't trouble Cassie, but she must watch out for the Entity, who will summon Glamrock Endo if he catches her here.

Cassie can find the first generator by going into the play equipment to the left of Daycare and wearing the Security Mask to operate another camera station in AR. She must go to CAM_5 first and quarantine Moon. The Entity appears after this, so she needs to quickly go to CAM_3, where she can quarantine Sun. This will move a cutout that was blocking a tunnel. This path leads up to the generator, which Cassie can switch on.

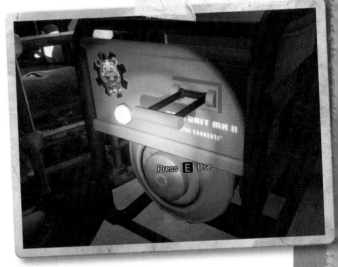

>>> Cassie drops down from here and can work her way around to another obstructed tunnel. Using the Security Mask, she can find another camera station. The items to quarantine this time are a cleaning robot on CAM_4 and then a sun symbol on CAM_2. The Entity spawns so she must remove the mask. When she puts it back on, it will unblock a tunnel that leads up to the other generator.

>>> DAYCARE

Cassie needs to return to Moon, so she drops down and heads back to the middle of the playpen, where she can take the stairs. Here, she can reboot Moon, turning him into Eclipse, who guides Cassie out of the playpen.

Cassie can now reach the theater, but the gate is closed, so she needs to use the mask to see the mother node. This search will trigger the Endoskeletons in this area: They act in the same way as in the main game, so Cassie has to watch them to stop them moving. However, they can't see her when she has the mask on.

The three child nodes here are a life buoy, a trolley, and a sun plushie— the last of these has to be released by completing a Faz-Wrench puzzle (upper wire first, lower wire second). The mother node puzzle will open the theater doors. Inside the theater, Cassie can explore upstairs—phase through the Captain Foxy poster in AR to find a collectible—but to leave, she must use the mask to find another camera station in AR. The three symbols to be quarantined are a sun on CAM_6, a moon on CAM_4, and a cleaning robot on CAM_2.

>>> An Endoskeleton comes crashing through the theater screen in AR, but there's no need to be scared! Cassie can go over to it, climb up the boxes to its mouth, and go inside. Cassie is terrified, but she takes off the Security Mask and realizes she's in a vent. The vent collapses and she lands back in Monty's Gator Golf, riding a gondola.

WALK-THROUGH

>>> CATWALK

The gondola track needs to be shifted by activating another mother node. These child nodes are challenging to find! First, Cassie needs to reach a turret, which, when fired, creates a path for her. Watch out for the slippery platform that drops—if Cassie falls in this area, it's game over! She turns left after the large gap that can only be crossed in AR, then keeps going until she finds the camera station. There's another gap that can be crossed in AR, and this leads to one child node—a pillar on its side.

Cassie returns to the camera station and uses another turret to shoot three targets and activate the bridge. She keeps going until she finds a gap she must cross in AR, which leads to a glitchy portal. This transports her to a place where the path forks. By taking the left fork with the camera station on it, she can locate another child node—a Monty Gator toy lying on the floor.

Cassie goes back to the fork and takes the right path, finding another turret and more targets to shoot. She crosses the bridge and takes the left path at another fork, passing a sign with two arrows on it. The next child node is at the end of a catwalk to nowhere, just past a camera station on the left, in the form of a chair that's toppled over.

>>> Cassie returns to the most recent fork, which leads to a pipe with another glitchy portal in it. This leads to a room where the Entity appears— but Helpy and Gregory put up a barrier to stop him. Cassie goes back to where she was and finds the final child node, a large storage box, at the end of the pipe. She returns to the mother node and solves the puzzle.

WALK-THROUGH

>>> MAINTENANCE ROOM

Before she can reach the maintenance room, Cassie has to complete another Faz-Wrench panel—the first with three wires. The timing is tricky on this one. The upper wire has to be completely filled first, then the bottom wire until it's just past the blue section, before filling the middle wire. Cassie can now ride the gondola out of here.

When Cassie gets off, she takes the stairs up to the maintenance room. There's another three-wire Faz-Wrench panel here. The upper and middle wires should be filled first, then the lower one. Cassie climbs the ladder and finds another Faz-Wrench panel. This one needs its upper wire filled to the top, then the middle wire, then the lower one. She then moves around to find a third panel—again, she needs to fill the upper and middle ones first.

Cassie sees Chica traveling on a conveyor, then she climbs up some boxes to get onto the conveyor. By going into AR, she can pass through the gate at the end—but then the Entity uses an inhibitor to remove her from AR! The inhibitor needs to be deactivated. Cassie can find another Faz-Wrench panel on the wall. This one needs the lower wire filled first, then the middle one— *then* a little more juice in the lower wire before doing the top wire.

>>> Cassie travels on a conveyor and encounters Chica, but is knocked off the conveyor and must head left. When Chica goes to block the path, Cassie avoids by retreating a little and then waiting for her to move away. At a camera station, Chica appears again, and Cassie distracts her by going to CAM_3 and using the intercom.

WALK-THROUGH

>>> CHICA'S BAKERY

As Cassie moves on, she'll see a red door on the left. This leads to the Chica's Feeding Frenzy arcade cabinet. The reward for completing this game is Chica's Voice Box—getting this is optional. There's another pathway to the right, and as soon as Cassie goes through this, Chica will return and the other path will no longer be available.

After escaping Chica, Cassie heads to the conveyor belt, where the inhibitor is. Disabling this allows Cassie to use the Security Mask again—but the Entity is very active around here, so Cassie should keep it off as much as possible. There's a mother node in the next area, but save time by getting two child nodes—a heart lollipop on a pile of junk and a Freddy bin next to a ramp—in this room. AR reveals a tunnel through the cupcake's mouth, and the other child node is another bin in a bathroom.

Cassie returns to the mother node and solves the puzzle. Another door opens, which leads to a door barred by police tape. This is the Server Room and can be accessed by wearing the Security Mask, which will be stuck to her head. Cassie walks through to find a camera station where she must quarantine symbols in this sequence: musical note (CAM_5), guitar (CAM_4), star (CAM_3), and lightning (CAM_2).

>>> In the next room, Cassie discovers the Entity *can* hurt her in here, despite what Helpy told her. She needs to quickly find another camera station and quarantine the symbols: star (CAM_2), lightning (CAM_3), and guitar (CAM_4). This enables her to escape. Phew!

>>> GLAMROCK SALON

Roxy is at the salon, and when she hears the voice of the boy who took her eyes on the Roxy-Talkie she goes to find him, locking the doors behind her. To unlock them, Cassie needs to disable the mother node. The first child node is a picture of Roxy lying propped on the floor, but after disabling that, the Security Mask becomes stuck again. She fixes this by disabling an inhibitor hidden nearby, where a stream of pink slime falls—it can be found by following the wires.

When Cassie comes to a fork, she should go left—the mirror on the crate is another child node. The mask gets stuck again, so she needs to walk back and disable another inhibitor. With the mask off, she goes over to the broken sign to find an oversize pair of scissors, which is the next child node. Cassie then needs to go to the camera station and quarantine these symbols: Roxy (CAM_5), Chica (CAM_3), scissors (CAM_4), and eye (CAM_6).

Walking on, Cassie can find the last node, a toy car, and disable the mother node. The now harmless Chica appears and Cassie can restore her Voice Box, if she has it, before moving on to the Faz-Wrench panel. The top wire on this must be filled last, after the other three.

Cassie passes through a flooded passage where Monty Gator lurks. She's safe while she's on a floating platform, so she should jump between them when Monty is farthest away. She tackles a Faz-Wrench panel where the lower two wires must be filled halfway before going to the top wire. Then there's another flooded tunnel and another Faz-Wrench panel, and Cassie must stand in the water to fix it. It's wise to wait for Monty to move back to the entrance before starting the panel. The upper two wires must be filled to just past the blue before working on the lower wire.

>>> Cassie gets out of the water just before it's electrified— but Monty is caught in it . . .

WALK-THROUGH

>>> ROXY'S RACEWAY

After failing to hail Gregory, Cassie heads into Roxy's Raceway and encounters a Faz-Wrench panel. Here the wires can be completed in any order, but one will need to be topped off after Cassie has filled them both. Roxy is here, but she can't see, so Cassie can move past her if she's quiet. However, Cassie needs to use Roxy to break down doors. She can go to the camera station and use CAM_5 and the intercom to send Roxy toward the door.

Moving forward, there's an AR camera station. Cassie can move Roxy by first using CAM_4 and the intercom, then when she gets there, moving to CAM_5. (Leaving the station and taking the mask off in between will de-spawn the Entity if he's around.) Roxy will break down another door.

>>> In the next area, a go-kart drives itself at Cassie, so she needs to run to her right. Then there's a Faz-Wrench panel, where the upper and lower wires need to be filled first, then the middle one. Roxy rocks up, demanding her eyes back: Cassie gets away but learns from Gregory that the sinkhole under the raceway can't be accessed without going to Bonnie Bowl and Fazer Blast . . .

>>> BONNIE BOWL

Cassie walks on and ends up in an office before finally reaching the staff area of Bonnie Bowl. There's another mother node here, and Cassie needs to use the Security Mask to make her invisible to the Lil' Music Men dotted around. On the first camera station she comes to, she should activate the intercom on CAM_3. This will move a group of Music Men away from a bowling shoe—which is the first child node.

Moving on and to the left, there's a Faz-Wrench panel: Cassie must fill the second wire to the end, then the fourth, then fill the third halfway, refill the second, and finally complete the upper wire. The mask is disabled as Cassie enters a storage room for arcade cabinets, so she must go right and disable an inhibitor. She can then go to the camera station and use the intercom on CAM_1. Quickly, she needs to put on the Security Mask and head for the back left corner of the room, where there's a child node in the form of a traffic cone.

Cassie's mask is disabled again. She needs to head right to another camera station and use the intercom on CAM_1, then run to the partially closed shutter and duck under it to avoid the Music Men. There's an inhibitor in here. With the Security Mask on, Cassie can find the bowling ball that is the next child node, then proceed to another Faz-Wrench panel. The upper wire needs to be completed first, then the lower one, then back to the upper.

>>> On the bowling alleys is another camera station where Cassie can use CAM_3 to draw the Music Men away, then disable the final child node—a bowling pin. She travels back to disable the mother node, before moving on in AR and deactivating another inhibitor. Finally, in a locker room, she can enter AR and go through an open vent.

>>> FAZER BLAST

Moving through a weird vortex, Cassie finds herself in an office and can make her way to Fazer Blast. She goes down the stairs and enters AR to go through a portal to the laser tag maze. Again, Cassie can't take off the mask, but before she can locate the inhibitor, she needs to use the mother node. She follows the wires to find the two child nodes—a sign and a mirror. It's smart to locate both *before* deactivating either of them, as the Entity spawns after doing the first one, and it's good to know exactly where the other one is!

Cassie can now tackle the mother node. The inhibitor is in the next tunnel, so Cassie can take off her mask again. Crawling through the hole in the junk, Cassie finds Freddy—but his head is missing. He chases Cassie, who must run as fast as she can. Watching the stamina is important here—don't let it get to the bottom!

>>> Cassie winds up in a room with an inhibitor, which she must approach quietly so the blind Freddy doesn't hear. She can operate the inhibitor and put on her mask, causing Freddy to vanish. Cassie proceeds to a vent where she must run to escape a Lil' Music Man before she can return to Roxy's Raceway. The final mother node is Roxy herself, who's trapped under a forklift. With the Security Mask on, Cassie can approach Roxy, and it turns out Roxy remembers her from her birthday party. Cassie deactivates her and can head down . . .

>>> THE SINKHOLE

Cassie emerges from the elevator into a tunnel, continues to walk, and turns left, reaching a cave. As she moves toward a lit-up area, her flashlight gets wet and no longer works. She goes inside a building and finds it's full of Fazbear merch. Deeper inside is Candy Cadet, who tells a story—Cassie must collect Faz-Coins to unlock the whole story.

Eventually Cassie comes to a Faz-Wrench panel where she needs to fill the bottom two wires to the end, then half fill the top one before the second one. She can then move on and drop down through a hole to find a computer. With the mask on, Cassie can use this to deactivate security, and the Entity is sucked inside it.

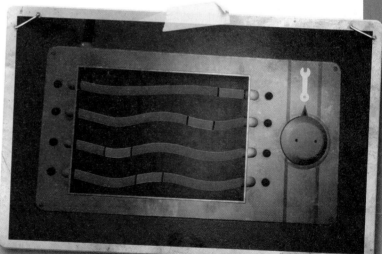

There's a Faz-Wrench panel on the forklift where the wires should be filled from the bottom up—one of the middle ones may need topping off. After completing this, the forklift smashes through the wall, and Cassie hears Gregory's voice . . . but it's not Gregory! It's the Mimic, who's been copying Gregory's voice. As he looms down on Cassie, Roxy arrives, distracting him long enough for Cassie to escape. The real Gregory speaks over the Roxy-Talkie and guides Cassie as the Mimic chases her.

Cassie must turn right twice, then go through a door and find a Faz-Wrench panel. This has to be solved with the Mimic in pursuit, though he does slow down a little. Cassie must tackle the upper wire first, then go to the bottom one and top off the upper wire . . .

>>> And that's it—the elevator takes Cassie out! But there are three possible endings . . .

WALK-THROUGH

ENDINGS

You get the **Standard Ending** if you complete the game as instructed on the previous page. Gregory— who was never at the Pizzaplex— tells Cassie the Mimic tricked her into going there and disabling the security to release it. But he tells Cassie, "We can't risk being followed," and lets the elevator fall with her in it . . .

The **Safe Spot Ending** appears if you follow Gregory's instructions at first, turning right twice, but instead of heading through the green-glowing passage in the caves, turn left and find a cutout of Freddy. Put on the Security Mask here to trigger a different ending sequence, where Cassie sees a seemingly happy picture of Gregory and Vanessa.

■ The **Scooper Ending** is the best one. This requires you to find four hidden cameras in certain camera stations. You need to look out for a black camera on the camera map, then cycle through the cameras to get the feed from the hidden one. Just looking at the hidden camera will unlock a door.

The hidden cameras are at the first station in Monty's Gator Golf; on the Catwalk, to the left of the vortex; at the sole camera station in Glamrock Beauty Salon; and the station in the bowling alley area of Bonnie Bowl. (And you don't have to do all these cameras on one playthrough. You can use Chapter Select to go back, unlock the cameras, and then go to the final chapter.)

When you play the final chapter again, a door you went through before will be blocked off and a different one will be open. Go this way until you reach a red button. Press it to set the Scooper against the Mimic!

Gregory:
Sorry. (elevator falls)

Cassie:
Gregory? Nooo!